To/

HAPPY
BIRTHDAY

Take a trip back in time to the year you were born, 1942.

Happy 80th Birthday - enjoy reminiscing.

Lots of love,

80 YEARS AGO BACK IN 1942

WORLD MAP

World Population

2.3 BILLION

America population

134.86MILLION

2022

World Population

7.9 BILLION

America population

329.5MILLION

MAJOR WORLD LEADERS

UK- PM WINSTON CHURCHILL

US- PRESIDENT FRANKLIN D. ROOSEVELT

RUSSIA/SOVIET UNION - JOSEPH STALIN

ITALY - PM BENITO MUSSOLINI

GERMANY - ADOLF HITLER

CANADA -PM WILLIAM LYON MCKENZIE KING

SOUTH AFRICA - PM FIELD MARSHALL JAN CHRISTIAAN SMUTS

MEXICO - MANUEL AVILA CAMACHO

JAPAN - FUMIMARO KONOE / HIDEKI TOLO

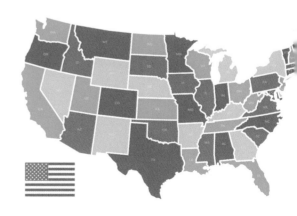

You Have Been Been Loved for

80 YEARS

Thats 960 months

4174 Weeks | 29,220 days

701,280 hrs

42,076,800 MINUTES

2,524,608,000 SECONDS

and counting...

80 & Fabulous

BARBERA JOAN STRIESAND

BORN IN NEW YORK 24TH APRIL

SINGER, ACTRESS AND DIRECTOR

SIR PAUL McCARTNEY

BORN IN LIVERPOOL 28TH

SINGER/SONGWRITER

SIR WILLIAM "BILLY" CONNOLLY

BORN GLASGOW 24TH NOV 1942

COMEDIAN, MUSICIAN AND TV PRESENTER

BOB HOSKINS

BORN IN BURRY UK 26TH OCT 1942

ACTOR

CAROLE KING

BORN NEW YORK 9TH FEB 1942

SINGER/SONGWRITER

HARRISON FORD

BORN IN CHICAGO 13TH JULY 1942

ACTOR

Oscars

Best Actor

Gary Cooper

Sargeant York

Box Office

8.3 million USD

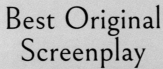

Best Original
Screenplay

Best Actress

Joan Fortaine

Suspicion

Box Office

4.5 million USD

Average cost of living

Cost of Living 1942

Average Cost of new house $3,770.00

Average wages per year $1,880.00

Average Monthly Rent $35.00 per month

Cost of a gallon of Gas 15 cents

Average Price for a new car $920.00

Bottle Coca Cola 5 cents

Top Ten Baby Names of 1942

Mary, Barbara, Patricia, Linda, Carol,

James, Robert, John, William, Richard

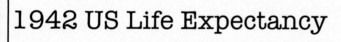

1942 US Life Expectancy

Males: 64.7 years, Females: 67.9 years

Voice of America (VOA)

The radio program Voice of America (VOA) was created as a tool to broadcast propaganda during WWII. It aired for the first time in February 1942. The primary aim was to combat Nazi propaganda and raise the spirits of the allied troops. When the war ended in 1945, VOA changed its focus to combating Soviet propaganda. It is still broadcast today; in 47 different languages and listened to by over 230 million people weekly.

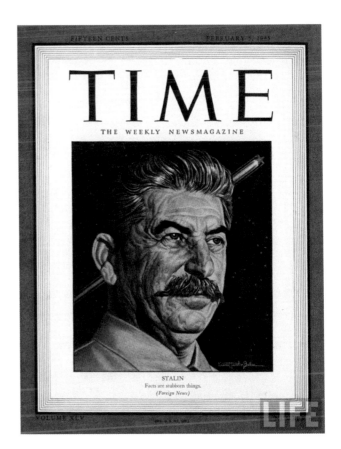

Time Magazine

Joseph Stalin was Time Magazine's Man of the year in 1943 (his second accolade from the magazine; the first was in 1939).

DID YOU KNOW?

Hawaii

During the war Hawaii introduced its own currency with a Hawaii stamp. The idea was that if Japan invaded their island, the U.S could say the money was worthless.

Penicillin

was in such short supply that it was recycled by extracting it from patients' urine.

Victory Speed Limit

In May of 1942, the US speed limit was reduced to 35mph. It was called the "Victory Speed limit".

Nobel Prize

Due to the war, there were no Nobel prizes awarded from 1940-42.

Disney Propaganda

Der Fuehrer's Face was the titled Disney Duck film created by Disney to help with the war effort. It was produced in 1942 and released in 1943. It was the only Donald Duck film to be nominated for an Oscar.

Bambi

This classic Disney film premiered on the 21st of August 1942. Based on the novel by Felix Salten, the film was a hit with the public and within the film industry; it was nominated for three Academy Awards.

By 1942, the war had been battling on for 3 years. The attack on Pearl Harbour on the 7th December 1941 was the event that caused the US to declare war on Japan. In 1941, most Americans heard about the declaration of war from a CBS radio announcement that interrupted a concert for NY Philharmonic.

Americans had already been impacted by the war, despite not formally joining until this point. The United States had provided support to allied nations. During 1941 manufacturers began diverting efforts from their own business to supporting the wartime needs of Europe. Raw materials such as steel, rubber, nylon, silk, oil, and fabrics were all in short supply. Automobile manufacturers started producing airplanes and tanks for the military. Fashion businesses began supplying uniforms for the military. The Japanese Imperial Army controlled the Dutch East Indies (today known as Indonesia) from 1942-45, which resulted in a nationwide shortage of rubber that impacted American production.

The war production board was set up in 1942 to coordinate companies who had redirected their business to help towards the war effort.

Before Franklin D. Roosevelt declared war on Japan, the US government began devising rationing measures to implement. In August 1941, President Roosevelt set up the Office of Price Administration (OPA). The purpose of this administration was to ensure fair pricing on particular goods and to implement rationing.

Americans received their first ration card in May 1942. The first card was called war ration book one. It was known as "the sugar book". Further ration cards were produced as the war progressed and shortages became more prevalent. Some ration cards featured stamps with various items such as tanks, guns, fruit, and drawings of airplanes.

Other items the OPA put on ration were automobiles, gasoline, fuel oil, coal, firewood, nylon, silk, as well as household staples including meat, butter, dairy, coffee, jams, jellies, lard, oil, and canned milk.

Citizens learned to adjust their lifestyle and do without. It was the united cause that helped boost morale when dealing with significant shortages of everyday goods. Wartime posters encouraged everyone to 'do their bit' and rationing was viewed as one of the ways that people on the home front could support the war effort.

Fuel restrictions were imposed depending on individual requirements. Most Americans received Class A rations, Americans with jobs essential to the war effort received Class B and C. Class A coupons allowed each car 150 miles for their jobs and 90 for family outings like running to the grocery store per month. Families who had relatives that lived a distance away couldn't visit as they had prior to the war. Class B and C allowed more gas and allowed for some flexibility in travel.

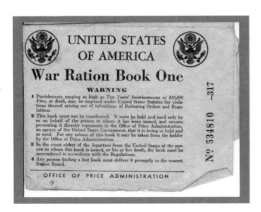

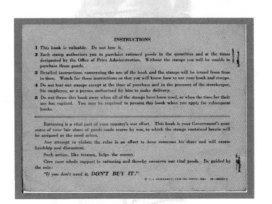

War Bonds

Defence Bonds became War Bonds in 1942. The sale of war bonds brought in more than $180 billion in revenue. Bonds were issued in denominations ranging from $10 to $1,000, depending on the year, and sold for 50% to 75% of their face value.

Investors paid less than the face value of the bonds initially and received the face value at maturity. Essentially, war bonds were considered zero-coupon bonds because they didn't pay interest or coupons throughout the year. At maturity, investors received the difference between the purchase price and the bond's face value.

Baby bonds are smaller than standard bonds in terms of par value or face value. Therefore, they were more affordable for retail investors. The bonds were also nontransferable - only the original purchaser could redeem them in the future. Originally, war bonds were ten years old, yielding 2.9%.

Congress extended the period during which interest could be earned so that bonds sold from 1941 to 1965 could accrue interest for forty years. Bonds issued interest for twenty years. War Bonds became known as Series E bonds after World War II. Series E bonds continued to be issued by the United States until 1980 when Series EE bonds replaced them.

I'm making bombs and buying bonds!

Buy VICTORY BONDS

The American Dream

"The premise of post-war industrial America is that the growth that we used to get by conquering other nations - enslaving their people and extracting their minerals - now we'd be able to get that growth internally through consumption. So we build the suburbs because if everyone's living in their own house, everyone's going to need their own dishwasher, their own washing machine, their own lawnmower, their own car, their own thing." Douglas Rushkoff

In 1945, the US emerged from World War II with optimism and a strengthened position as a key world power. WWII decimated Europe, China, the Soviet Union, and Japan. The war cost all the fighting nations dearly. America suffered the tragic loss of over 400,000 military personnel. Despite this America was in a better position than the rest of the world and quickly set out with a plan to solidify its position as a leading superpower.

Changes in society in the late 1940s completely changed the way we live today. There were 17 million new jobs created, the nation's industrial productivity increased, and corporate profits surged. Naturally, the American Dream was not a novel concept. The country was built on this vision. What was different was that it was becoming mainstream. This was driven by a new ideology - consumption.

Life at home

The attack on Pearl harbour in 1941 caused a seismic shift in the life of all US citizens. America found itself unprepared; resources were scrambled to retaliate, young men and fathers enlisted leaving their families to be led by the wife, labour shortages opened up work opportunities for married women (many of the roles previously being unthinkable for women to do), propaganda ensured that the war effort on the home front supported the forces abroad. Given the complex diversity of the U.S., it would be impossible to provide an accurate one size fits all description of family life. The changes set in force following the victory in 1945 would affect the way of life socially, culturally, and economically.

The nation became urbanised. Many families move from rural areas to work in the new factories in the cities. Many married women continued their employment after the war ended. This allowed a significant increase in the standard of daily living. People wanted to buy their own home and to fill it with state of the art labour saving products such as washing machines, hoovers, ovens & refrigerators. The American Dream became a viable reality for many and a wish for all.

Entertainment - Radio & TV

During the '40s Americans on average listened to the radio for 5 hours per day. The first practical TV sets were demonstrated and sold to the public at the 1939 World's Fair in New York. The sets were very expensive and New York City had the only broadcast station. In 1947, President Harry Truman's state of the union address and the baseball World Series was televised. A year later, CBS and NBC networks started 15-minute nightly newscasts. In the late 1940s, there were 98 commercial television stations in 50 large cities. By 1949, 100,000 TV sets were being purchased every week. By the early 1950s, Americans watched television 5 hours a day, replacing radio entertainment in just a few years.

Food

Rations at home and K rations abroad changed the eating habits of people. Ground beef took less ration and so meatloaf, spaghetti and meat rolls became popular - and have remained so. In rural areas people still hadn't adopted frozen food however changes in supply meant that local rural shops advertised frozen food and these were adopted with surprising favour.

"Foods formerly manufactured solely for army use will now be put on the civilian market," announced American Cookery magazine in 1946. Many convenience foods were first developed in the '40s.

Transport

for the first time in history, production stopped for nearly 4 years. From 1942-46 production of domestic cars was halted. This was the only period of time when automobile production stopped completely. No cars were manufactured after 1942 due to the advent of World War II. Production for civilians did not resume until 1946.

Sugar ration queue

American home

Levittown

These prototype American suburbs were built following WWII for returning veterans. In total 7 communities were initially constructed by real estate developer William Levitt. To keep the costs low they were prefabricated and each house was almost identical. The first Levittown was built on Long Island between 1947-51 and was followed by developments in Pennsylvania, New Jersey, Puerto Rico, and Maryland. Levitt only sold to white buyers, excluding African Americans despite the fact that housing segregation was deemed constitutionally illegal in 1948.

Films

THE TALK OF THE TOWN

No. 1236_778

When Nora says to the professor "he is as whiskered as the Smith Brothers", she is referring to a brand of cough drops manufactured by the Smith Brothers. The bottles had illustrations of the brothers on each bottle, both sporting full beards. This brand was the most popular cough drop brand for over a century.

No. 1236_779

BAMBI

Walt Disney produced many animated movies. Bambi was his personal favorite. Well known for disrupting the tradition, Walt insisted on children providing the voices for the characters instead of the usual adults mimicking children.

CASABLANCA

No. 1236_780

Due to wartime restrictions during the filming of Casablanca, the crew was not able to film at the airport at night. They had to improvise with a soundstage and cut out airplanes to provide a perspective for the overall staging.

Films

WWII Impact on the Film Industry

Before the outbreak of war in Europe 1939, American films were primarily musicals and light-hearted entertainment in the form of romances and drama. However, as the war crept closer to home, the film industry became impatient to reflect the fascism at home and abroad.

Following the Japanese attack on Pearl Harbour, the film industry focused its voice and power on helping their Government at war.

From 1942-to 1945 the film industry focused its resources on the war effort. It was effective in influencing the social, political, and military opinions of millions of Americans proving a vital tool in winning the war.

- Casablanca starring Humphrey Bogart, Ingrid Bergman & Claude Rains

- The Talk of The Town starring Cary Grant, Jea Arthur & Edgar Buchanan

- Mrs. Miniver starring Greer Garson, Walter Pidgeon & Richard Ney

- Road to Morocco starring Bob Hope, Dorothy Lamour & Anthony Quinn

- Woman of The Year starring Spencer Tracy, Katharine Hepburn & William Bendix

- Now, Voyager starring Bette Davis, Paul Henreid & Claude Rains

- Holiday Inn starring Bing Crosby, Fred Astaire & Marjorie Reynolds

- Saboteur Sterling Norman Lloyd, Priscilla Lane & Robert Cummings

- Across the Pacific starring Mary Astor, Humphrey Bogart & Sydney Greenstreet

- For Me and my Gal starring Judy Garland, Gene Kelly & George Murphy

Music

Harry Lillis "Bing" Crosby Jr.

American Singer, Comedian and Actor. The first multimedia star.

Born 3rd May 1903 in Washington USA.

Biggest hit was the recording of Irving Berlin's White Christmas, first broadcast on Christmas day 1941, it sold over 50 million copies, Topping the charts in three different years, 1942, 45 and 47

Alton Glenn Miller was an American Big Band Trombonist, Composer and Band Leader in the 40s Swing era. The Best selling Artist from 1939-1942, Miller scored 16 number ones and 69 top 10 hits, beating Elvis who had 38 top 10s and the Beatles who had 33 top 10s.

No 1's

Find out what the number 1 was when you
were born. Check the table below.

3rd Jan-1 Jan	Bless You	Ink Spots
3rd Jan-6th Feb	Chattannooga Choo Choo	Glenn Miller
7th Feb-13th Feb	A String of Pearls	Glenn Miller
14th Feb-20th Feb	Blues in the Night	Woody Herman
21st Feb-27th Feb	A String of Pearls	Glenn Miller
28th Feb-8th May	Moonlight Cocktail	Glenn Miller
9th May-19t	Tangerine	Jimmy Dorsey
20th Jun-17th Jul	Sleepy lagoon	Harry James
18th Jul-11th Sep	Jingle Jangle Jingle	Kay Kyser
12th Sep-30th Oct	Ive got a Gal in	Glenn Miller
31st Oct-1st Jan	White Christmas	Bing Crosby

Fashion

The war brought significant changes to everyday fashion. The style throughout the 40s was defined by WWII. The scarcity of resources led to shorter skirts, less formality, and in general a shift in the 'required' outfits for particular situations. Pre-war it would be expected for a man to have a work suit/outfit, weekend wear, and a 'Sunday finest' outfit for worship. The casual suit became acceptable in all situations and this remained in place post-1945.

Women's wardrobes were similarly slimmed down. The 'Make do and Mend' campaign was successful in ensuring that clothes were repaired and reused. The military uniform also had a significant influence. Many men and women wore their uniforms off and on duty. Brides even had bridesmaids in military uniform on their wedding day. The restrictions did not appear to hamper the desire to look stylish. Women in particular employed ingenious ways to style themselves within these restrictions on resources. In 1942, the American War Production Board issued Regulation L-85 which restricted the materials and methods manufacturers could use to make clothing to control resources needed for the war.

While the fashion houses in Paris all but came to a complete stop, the American fashion industry bloomed; heavily influenced by Hollywood. During World War II, American fashion designers were the key players in the industry. Post-1945 Paris reclaimed her title. Dior dazzled with the 'New Look' in 1947 however American and British designers both enjoyed more prominence

Fashion

& influence than they had previously.

Intuitive styles were being developed by American designers like Adrian, Claire McCardell, and Pauline Trigère. The change in design ethos allowed a lighter, less structured form than the traditional Paris house fashions. Popular styles were a wedge silhouette with wide shoulders, a narrow waist, a single-pleated A-line skirt. Due to the Regulation L-85 restriction on the use of fabric, the hemlines were raised to knee length.

Many men wore military uniforms, but those who didn't faced the same clothing restrictions women did. Many men chose to wear their older 1930s style suits to support the war effort by conserving material. The suits designed in the early 40s were more slimline, without vests or cuffs to save on fabric. Ties were made from wool and tied in Windsor knots. The War Production Board (WPB) became the nation's premier clothing consultant in the spring of 1942. They influenced civilian apparel by dictating the conservation of cloth and metal, changing the style - especially for women. Dependence on fewer materials led to the two-piece bathing suit. Nieman Marcus called them "patriotic chic."

Childhood

Children's experiences of the early 40s would have differed according to a variety of factors; geographical location, social & economic status, and race. Over the course of the war 5 million "war widows" were left to try to manage their households alone. The labor shortage (from men being sent off to fight in the war) opened up many opportunities for women to enter the workplace. This, in turn, created challenges for childcare. Attracted by the abundant availability of paid positions many young people left school early to take employment and contribute towards household expenses (teenage school leavers grew from 1 million to 3 million causing the federal government to turn a blind eye to the laws curtailing childhood employment. For some the war would have been devastating; families left without fathers & brothers. Regardless of the personal impact, the entire country had to endure sacrifice in one way or another.

Throughout the war, children were encouraged through propaganda to contribute to the war effort. Posters in schools and community halls showed conscientious children doing their bit' by collecting scrap materials for ammunition, bombs, and military vehicles. Bedtime stories came with messages to buy war bonds and hate the enemy.

While fear and personal sacrifice prevailed, the war also brought a sense of excitement. The rallying of troops, the community spirit, the collection of metals helped fight the enemy. Children of the 40s might remember their mothers saving and reusing grease from the frying pan. They might also remember saving tin foil, flattening cans and of course, many families created a victory garden in the backyard.

Children of the 40s grew up in a time of profound transformation and upheaval. Not only the impact of war but also the US was changing its economy from one that relied on agriculture to one of industry in large cities. The end of the war and the transformation in the economy led to the birth of a renewed American Dream and this change impacted the future of the country for every one of its citizens.

Toys

As with every other aspect of life in the first half of the '40s, the war heavily impacted the toys that children played with. Unsurprisingly they had a heavy war focus. Games around this time included "Bombs over Toyko!", Guns and military toys were in the hands of almost every little boy.

The production of toys was limited due to limited material supplies - metal and rubber being essential in military production. Small girls played with dolls, played house, and pretended to be moms since life was still very traditional.

In general, toys were beginning to become more advanced. However, shortages hindered this until the late 1940s. Electronic games came to market; very basic and not what kids today would term electronic. Innovative toys included the slinky, the magic 8 ball, Circus Sam the Balancing Man, silly putty and shoot the moon.

98 cent toys were popular pocket money toys. Other notable toys include; a crystal radio set, portable electric phonograph, steel cars and trucks, doctors/nurses playsets, WWII model airplane kits, WWII Rosie O'Neill Kewpie doll, and tiddlywinks. Monopoly was the most popular family board game. Many toy producers tried to create the 'next monopoly and games such as Chutes & Ladders (introduced by Milton Bradley in 1943), scrabble, Rummikub and Clue were developed. As a family, we played card games, dice, pick-up sticks, noughts and crosses, and Jacks. Despite the huge advances in technology it's reassuring to see that many of these are still enjoyed by families today.

Slinky

1940- Slinky Richard James, a mechanical engineer, was working to design springs that could keep sensitive ship equipment steady at sea. He accidentally knocked into his shelf of samples, causing his invention to gracefully "walk down." Slinky saw sales soar through the next few decades, and still enjoys favorite toy status

Christmas on the home front

Despite the fact that the war didn't allow for a holiday, Americans at home tried to keep the holiday as normal as possible, particularly for the children. Labor shortages affected the supply of Christmas trees. The scarcity of railroad space made it difficult to get the tress to market. Americans rushed to buy artificial trees in the absence of real trees. A 5ft tree could be purchased for 75 cents. The traditional outdoor lights were among the war casualties. There were no lights or trees lit in the streets, community blackouts and dim-outs to control the use of fuel meant it was a dimmer affair than usual.

People became creative in making their own ornaments. Internationally designed ornaments, especially oriental and German-made were disposed of. Magazines offered creative ways to create your own stylish ornaments out of non-priority war materials like paper, string, and natural objects such as pine cones. An ingenious way of giving the trees a snow-covered effect was to mix a box of Lux soap powder with water and brush the branches of the tree.

Fewer men at home meant fewer people for the Santa role. The community rallied to make sure the Santa visits were still possible for the children. Women even substituted Santa at Saks Fifth Avenue in New York City. It was a way people could keep things as close to normal as possible. Traditions become a lifeline in a time of uncertainty.

Despite the fact that wartime income was high for many during the war, shortages meant the availability of products was limited. Many people gave presents they had made themselves. Although clothing wasn't rationed, restrictions did apply and availability was reduced.

Travel was limited due to fuel shortages. Families saved up their coupons to allow for extra food for Christmas dinner. Post-war the Christmas of 1946 was a welcome return to normality. It was celebrated with wild abandon. Households around the country were determined to make up for the previous 3 years of scarcity.

Macy's department store NY Christmas 1941- the last Christmas before WWII rations affected supply.

Family enjoying Christmas dinner - weeks of rations coupons saved to allow a normal Christmas Dinner.

Post-war Christmas welcomed the return of real Christmas trees.

World Events 1942

Actress Carole Lombard is killed

An American film actress is killed on a TWA flight alongside her mother and 16 others. She was on tour promoting War Bonds. Recently Carole was nominated as the 16th Greatest Actress of all time.

Henry Ford

Ford is granted a patent for a plastic car. The benefit is it is 30% lighter than a regular car.

War Relocation Authority

Franklin D. Roosevelt, President of the U.S implements the Executive Order creating the WRA that relocates 120,000 Japanese and people with Japanese ancestry living in America, many for the duration of the war.

WWII - Nazi, the Reichstag

The last meeting of the Reichstag dissolves itself giving absolute power to Adolf Hitler. Hitler is given the authority and control of the life and death of every German citizen.

Operation Typhoon

On January 7th Germany failed to take Moscow.

Declaration of the UN

In January, 26 nations sign the declaration of the UN. The treaty was signed in Washington, D.C. It held each nation to adhere to the Atlantic charter.

Pilot Helmet Schenk

Heinkel test pilot, Helmut Schenk is successful in his mission to escape from an aircraft using an ejection seat.

Singapore falls to Japan

Academy Awards

14th Academy awards are held in Los Angeles. The Best Picture goes to 'How Green Was My Valley'.

World events

Princess Elizabeth

The young Princess signs up for War Service.

Anne Frank

The first entry in Anne Franks diary is recorded as June 12th.

JUN

Nuclear Reactor

He first Nuclear accident in history is recorded on the 23rd June. The nuclear reactor L-IV explodes causing a reactor fire in Leipzig.

Anne Frank

Records show Anne Frank's family fled into hiding on the 6th of July. They hid in the attic above her father's office in a warehouse in Amsterdam.

AUG

Radio controlled Torpedos

Hedy Lamarr and George Antheil register a patent for a radio-controlled torpedo. The patent is granted however, it is not in use until 1962 during the Cuban Missile Crisis.

Plutonium

On August 20th at the Metallurgical Laboratory, Plutonium is isolated for the first time.

Battle of Midway

American naval success, marks an important turning point in the Pacific War.

Bambi

April 12th - Bambi is released.

World Events 1942

Zofia Kossak-Szczucka

Polish writer and head of the underground organization Front for the Rebirth of Poland published a book to protest the mass murder of the Jewish population in German-occupied Poland.

OXFAM founded

The Oxford Committee for Famine Relief is founded on the 31st July.

WAVES

WAVES (Women Accepted for Volunteer Emergency Service) as part of the US naval reserve, is signed into law.

WAFS

The Women's Auxiliary Ferrying Squadron (WAFS) is established in the U.S.

Operation Pluto

The river Medwey is used to test the plan to construct oil pipelines under the English Channel.

JULY

Luxembourgish general strike

Protests about forced conscription take place in Luxembourg. It was a display of passive resistance and was met with force by German authorities. 21 strikers were sentenced to death.

US Scrap days

Beginning October 1942, the U.S government began a Scrap days campaign. Encouraging people to donate scrap items that could be repurposed and used in the War effort.

World events

SEP

A-4 Rocket launch

The first man made object to reach space is the A-4 Rocket. Launched in Germany, it flew 147 kilometres with an altitude of 84.5 Km.

OCT

Casablanca

Premiere of the now classic film, takes place in the Hollywood Theatre in New York City.

NOV

Alaskan Highway

Also known as the Alcan Highway, the Alaskan Highway, connecting Alaska to Canada, was finally completed, however, it was not in use until a year later 1943.

The Holocaust - Oct

Political figureheads in the U.K hold a public meeting to display their anger over the persecution of the Jewish people at the hand of the Nazi regime.

Enigma retrieval

Brave British soldiers board a sinking U boat (U-559) while it sinks to retrieve it's Enigma machine along with the codebooks.

Times Square

For the first time since it began its much-loved tradition, the Times Square Ball was not dropped at midnight. Instead, there was a one-minute silence, followed by a recording of bells ringing.

Manhattan Project

At the University of Chicago, a team of scientists initiate the first self-sustaining nuclear chain reaction.

Inventions from the early 40s

The 1940s can reasonably be referred to as one of the most significant decades of the past century. Undeniably the war impacted in a way that would affect generations to come however it was also the technology that was created as a direct result of the war that would go on to change our lives forever. The events of the 1940s are still remembered today and the inventions that resulted have influenced society to the present day.

Aerosol can

The concept of an aerosol goes back to the 1790s, the first patent granted in 1927 however it wasn't until 1941 that the aerosol can was first put to efficient use by Lyle Goodhue & William Sullivan who are widely credited as inventors of the modern spray can. It was created during WWII as a means to kill malaria carrying bugs for soldiers.

Biomimicry

Velcro

A fascinating story of inspiration. Inventor George de Mentral was out walking his dogs and noticed how effectively the burrs attached to his dog. A flash of inspiration resulted in his developing velcro-an amazing multi-purpose material

CBS & Peter Goldmark pioneered a system which transmitted an image in each of the 3 primary colours. Their TV was based on John Logie Bairds designs.

Mobile Phones

Surprised? While the first commercially viable phone didn't come into existence until 1983 it was way back in 1947 that T&T proposed the allocation of radio-spectrum frequencies with the intention of widespread telephone service. Bell Laboratories that introduced the idea of cellular comms in 1947 with police car technology.

The Jeep

Was designed in 1940 in just 18 hrs by Karl Probst. Production of the first prototype took just 72 days.

The Z3 - May 12th 1941

Konrad Zuse The Z3 was the world's first working programmable, fully automatic digital computer. It was also the first computer-controlled by software. The computer itself was built with 2,600 relays implementing a 22-bit word length that operated at A clock frequency of approximately 4-5 Hz.

Inventions from the early 40s

Atomic Bomb

"I am become Death, the destroyer of worlds." The words that theoretical physicist, J. Robert Oppenheimer, reportedly said after he saw the result of his invention. The quote comes from a Hindu famous scripture, also said to be a mistranslation. Without a doubt, the atomic bomb and its destructive power were life changing, impacting the course of WWII, the coming Cold War and the course of our history.

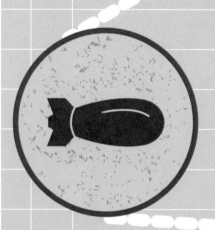

The Kidney Dialysis Machine

Willem Johan Pim Kolff was a pioneer in the field of hemodialysis and field of artificial organs. During WWII he made major discoveries in the field of kidney dialysis; the result of which would go on to save countless lives.

The Juke Box

The first jukebox was in play in 1890s, however the jukebox as you will think of it didn't appear until the 1940s. During the 40's it's estimated that two thirds of all records in USA were played on jukeboxes, such was their popularity.

Microwave

Percy Spence is the man that brought the microwave over into existence in 1947. The invention was actually based off of radar technology that was created during the war. However, it was still far from the microwave that you know today. The countertop friendly microwave did not make its way to the market until 1967.

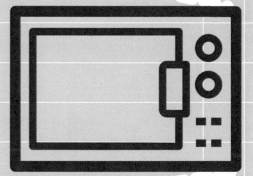

"OF COURSE I CAN!"

I'm patriotic as can be—
And ration points won't worry me!"

VICTORY WAITS ON **YOUR** FINGERS—

KEEP 'EM FLYING, MISS U.S.A.

The enemy wants to know what you know...

Keep it under your
STETSON

"Good Work, Sister
WE NEVER FIGURED YOU COULD DO A MAN-SIZE JOB!"

AMERICA'S WOMEN HAVE MET THE TEST!

For your country's sake today-

For your own sake tomorrow

GO TO THE NEAREST RECRUITING STATION OF THE ARMED SERVICE OF YOUR CHOICE

I'm Proud... my husband _wants_ me to do my part
SEE YOUR U. S. EMPLOYMENT SERVICE
WAR MANPOWER COMMISSION

KEEP PUNCHING..

EVERY DAY!
Your LABOR-MANAGEMENT PRODUCTION COMMITTEE

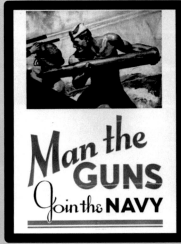

Man the GUNS
Join the NAVY

Pitch in and Help!

JOIN THE WOMEN'S LAND ARMY
OF THE U.S. CROP CORPS

A LIFETIME EDUCATION *FREE*
FOR HIGH SCHOOL GRADUATES WHO QUALIFY
U.S. CADET NURSE CORPS

When you ride ALONE you ride with Hitler!
Join a Car-Sharing Club TODAY!

Millions of troops are on the move...
Is YOUR trip necessary?

Women in the war
WE CAN'T WIN WITHOUT THEM

Keep us flying!
BUY WAR BONDS

Jenny on the job
Wears styles designed for Victory

1778   1943
AMERICANS will _always_ fight for liberty

PLAN TODAY
Build Tomorrow
WITH WAR BONDS THRU PAY ROLL SAVING

I WANT YOU
for the **U.S. ARMY**
ENLIST NOW

Advertising

During the war years of the '40s, advertisers played a crucial role in mobilizing the home front. Every citizen, including children, was affected by the propaganda. Advertising blended with propaganda and proved to be a crucial weapon in the American arsenal. From basic military recruitment, the raising of funds through the successful Buy War Bonds campaigns to the rally to raise morale on the home front; enlisting women to take on 'men's' vacant roles, and the promotion of Victory gardens. Just looking at the posters on the previous pages gives a feel for how emotive and effective these would have been in the midst of a war.

Advertisers were at the forefront of the expansion of consumerism after World War II. Their campaigns helped drive consumption to unprecedented levels. While the war boosted the economy, people had endured years of hardship and sacrifice. The United States emerged from the war as a leading superpower and enjoyed an optimism that would fuel expansion. This was unlike other countries that were browbeaten by the war and would take years to rebuild infrastructure & economies. With the economy shifting from agricultural to industrial, women who had entered the workplace as a necessity found that they wanted to remain there, boosting family finances. In post-war American society, advertisers played a major role in creating a consumer culture.

The timing was extremely fortunate. All industries were innovating and the possibilities seemed endless. In the mid-40s, advertising was primarily print-based, but after a few short years, it would be dominated by TV advertising.

Original 40s adverts - a picture truly tells a thousand words...

The original post-war adverts -on the following page- show the explosion of new products to market. Consumers were desperate to spend. The higher household income allowed families to improve their quality of life. Housewives wanted convenience foods and household items, husbands wanted to provide their families with the best of the best. This winning situation had advertisers rubbing their hands together. They were at the forefront of the expansion of consumerism. Through the campaigns they led, consumerism reached unprecedented levels.

• "More Doctors smoke Camels than any other cigarette" Leading Brand Camles enjoys a lack of advertising regulation. Smoking advertising was made illegal in the 1960s.

• Food & Drink

Following years of rationing and sacrifice, food companies developed new products quickly, supported by a strong economy and a country in desperate need of variety and color. Within the food industry, advertisers played a vital role in shifting consumer demands and buying patterns.

1. Pillsbury pancake mix. In 1949, the company introduced a national baking competition, which came to be known as the Pillsbury Bake-Off; it was nationally broadcast on CBS for many years.

2. Royal Tapioca pudding

3. Cheez-it - founded in 1921 by Green & Green originally marketed as "a baked rarebit"

4. Jujy fruits candies - originated in 1920 and produced by Ferrera Candy company. These were popular sweets to have at the movies.

5. Rice Krispies / Variery cornflakes. Traditional breakfast was being replaced by more convenient options. Cereal consumption boomed in the late 40s

6. Swifts Brookfield was founded by Gustav Franklin Swift in the late 19th century. Quick to innovate meat products for convenience, this company enjoyed significant success through the 1940s.

7. Brachs Chocolate Cherries was founded in 1904 by Emil J. Brach. The company once owned the largest candy store in the world. The company folded in 2003, missing its centennial.

8. Hamms Beer - first brewed in 1865 in Minnesota. While it is no longer an independent brewing company, the brand is still sold under the Hamms brand in certain markets.

9. Nescafe instant coffee. First developed in the late 1930s, Nescafe was released in 1940. It was an immediate success, the year's supply sold out in just 2 months. WWII had a significant effect on this progress as supply chains were severely disrupted. By 1941, NESCAFÉ had turned around this situation, and instant coffee was included in every soldier's emergency ration. NESCAFÉ was added to CARE packages in 1945, which was a turning point in NESCAFÉ history since it boosted demand to new heights.

10. 7-UP was first formulated in 1929, Missouri. By the late 1940s, it was the third most popular drink in the world. (By the 1990s it had fallen to the 8th most popular drink).

11. Coca-Cola - In 1943, the United States government requests access to Coca-Cola for its troops. Robert Woodruff pledges to provide Coke to the military for a nickel regardless of what it costs the Company to produce the product. From 1943-45, 64 portable bottling plants were distributed between Asia, Europe, and North Africa, bottling more than 5 million bottles of coca-cola.

12. Beech-Nut Gum

• Simoniz for floors - "Don't tell Jim. Why he'd say I was lazy..."

Looking at the ads might shock today's consumers. The difference in the acceptable language shows that advertisers and the public in the '40s held very different views than today's society.

• Firestone appliances. This advert shows the plethora of new products for the home & garden that became available in the later half of the '40s.

ROYAL
TAPIOCA PUDDINGS

Lighter pancakes are here! (Pillsbury Pancakes)

Pillsbury
PANCAKE MIX

look SHARP
feel SHARP
be SHARP

use Gillette
Blue Blades

Firestone

For a HUMMER of a SUMMER!...

GET NEW Mobiloil

See Your Mobilgas Dealer

According to a recent nationwide survey:
MORE DOCTORS SMOKE CAMELS
THAN ANY OTHER CIGARETTE

Camels

First in the Service...

They've Got What it Takes

Camels

Automatic Beyond Belief!

SENSATIONAL NEW

Sunbeam
RADIANT CONTROL
TOASTER

6 DELIGHTFUL Cereals
for extra energy—
Kellogg's VARIETY

"THE GRAINS ARE GREAT FOODS" — W. K. Kellogg

Flavor
makes all the difference
in the world!

Beech-Nut
GUM

The legal stuff

Made in the USA
Monee, IL
08 February 2022

90796184R00026